I

WAKE

IN

HALF DREAM

❖

IMELDA O'REILLY

❖

Belfast
LAPWING

First Published by Lapwing Publications
c/o 1, Ballysillan Drive
Belfast BT14 8HQ

Copyright © Imelda O'Reilly 2004
20/04/05

British Library Cataloguing in Publication Data.
A catalogue record for this book is available from
the British Library.

Set in Aldine 721 BT
by
Winepress Services

ISBN 1 898472 97 1

ACKNOWLEDGEMENTS

'Emilita' & 'The Faery Glen'

Emilita and the Faery Glen
was produced by
DeadalusTheatre Company
Off Broadway,
at the Clemente Soto Velez Cultural Center
in Manhattan, New York City, 2001
Directed by Imelda O'Reilly

I

WAKE

IN

HALF DREAM

❖

IMELDA O'REILLY

❖

To:

Edward and Winifred Caffrey

and

Anna Hayles

ROOTS I FLY

Had I set down roots in my mind cottage, or the space of my dreams; I would be different — the lane is narrow and the cottage seated silent in the countryside wide and green spinning its web round my thoughts, under the skin of ideas, running. There I stood those first years ferocious with wide eyes, eyes of wild wonder where the hips of childhood stood round mysterious hedges hiding.

The water fills with dream and dark hope lingering across the sodden fields across the blundering sky in my mind chain hooked in the wish well water mad with thoughts of landscapes and houses with tongues slithering scandalous silver, to take the consciousness of stream that flows and whistle blows a wonder conker in the openness of space the sky a billowing womb restlessness in huge hunger.

Until I shoved dug the outer reaches of mind roots running haywire in a boundless vast terrifying space.

And the notion descends journey a mind voyage gawking straight in the face of ROOTS I fly beyond stream, landscape violent, stitching the space between time, dream and half dream that clings SKIN and the stream doesn't explain the dream coming close and closer to the flesh, the bones and those roots I fly I, I fly I, I
fly
DEEP

IFDREAM

If dreams are lonely
what barren landscape
hushes toward me
whisper.
Memory lingers, trapped
seam of dark night.

Effusing mention as a fog descend
no no landscape clung
but I lie stretched suspended
in nothingness
of my body
Ohhhh body in bed with a blistered

dream.

Yes,
If dreams are lonely
what barren landscape
all that flesh summoned,
by the whip of time
determine my meaning
of a life
drunken moments
surrender
on the sword;
laughter and sorrow
mixed.

Ohhh the pong
comes in the whiffing daylight of day
sudden black dot.

Remember
a lost thought in the night
a frightened body;

Kiss
Oh kiss
by the steal
Of oh
dark lonely night
Ifdream.

LEMON SMILES

Colour falls
black of black
trim on,
wintered two lips
flow condemned
beyond scurry
where lillies once grew,
I drew you perfectly
conjured throes
billow my shadow
fills the open jar,
who sits
between red thighs
I saw lemons
fall sweet
so deft from some
tree I knew not soft.
Hangs out
rushes could not conceal
white naked bodies
sang velvet morning tunes,
skinned
I lay open
hay blows
secret moulds grew
tempted on waves
discover the cold rush.
Streams a golden syrup
steam quiet,
under tinker bells
I, naked on breasts
wonderwollyeyed
hung on the
cleaver of your heartdrop
no love
love without smiles
love
love
love
love h a n g s on an
a
x
e

TWIGS OF SCENT

twigs

        of

                scent

magpie mountain, go before eternal ear of banishment beyond the memory of mouth. Forward, he trods   clip — clop, singing balloons as they bloat thru a sky of blood. His pouted beak wanders the salt of the earth, hissing about, shovelling thru shells collected hidden. I trundle before the caped gown, mouth wide open smashed between pillows of wonder where the royal grain of truth lies sealed in the pit of ocean mystery. But the place of meet between magpie mountain & ocean of mystery billows between twigs of scent. Low beholden in middle of citadel bursts open a giant flame of movement simmering a kettle blows its bubble coughing in the blackened night sky. Ask promise, before the gift essence of scent a pebble rain in between pine needles, aniseed balls fall as snow gently melds the sky of blood to trace silhouette. Mad ocean of mystery chase the capture to reinvent a falling under the rushing sky where all reality tumbles together, fuses sipssss. Magpie mountain chase the catch of his wings in rugged darkness whereupon he met hollow sinking, afraid he crushes only to brush upon a lonely aniseed ball who whispers in his ear slow, as he listens before he hits the sodden ground.

WHERE COBWEBS SLEEP

Gummed along
threadbare slopes
I arrive
to sojourn in
your frozen land
among stuffed dummies,
where warped encasements
lie trapped, fossiled,
buried,
in your mind's tomb.

Discover bitten off
iced creatures of broken enchantment
stuffed as dolls,
storms chopped
without scent
of idle truth
to swallow through,
windows of thought
no birth.

Between money or art
you stand a rag doll
wrapped in garments of wedding,
where cobwebs sleep,
lost in memory
dressed in fear
not breathing truth.
Piling the pebbles
of frozen children
locked in glass,
locked in glass
l
o
c
k
e
d
in
g
l
a
ss

THE POETRY LIBRARY

THE FISH LOEM

I did I did I did
I did I did
catch a fish alive,

stands
stems
frosted eye
dementia.

Gladly
you bake
on my languid tongue
horrid.

Crooked
you take
all wonder endowed
slap.

A ballad begins
Chinese duel,
benign
no language no nooks.

I did I did
catch a fish alive
but it swings
a butcher a rose.

Replacement sin
given the boot
under compliment
undergo.

Naked blister
frolics against
the flesh to God knows where
dependent lullaby rocks,

pasted confusion twists out
emotion crumbles
languid on stick
stolen.

50 bags full 'n more
crawls a ghostly flaw

amongst churns
sting,
uncloister unclose
a disguised sniper
you smile.

Guillotine bodies
used
float in a curry
crushed brutal
entropy
love their tangoed bomb.

Ohhhh, love
love love's the tango bomb.

I did
I did
I did
catch a fish alive

bemose

muse

glimpse
a
crumb.

EMILITA AND THE FAERY GLEN

Ohhhh to go to the Faery Glen,
the wild with child Faery Glen,
where the trees sleep gold and the grass never grows old,
ohhhhh to go to the Faery Glen.

Where the Sun Goddess Emilita sleeps with the King of Mist,
and the rain it comes and tinkles onnnn
under the river and under the sea
the wild child conceived under a honey tree.
Ohhh   to go   to the Faery Glen
the wild with child   Faery Glen
where the trees sleep gold
and the grass never grows old
Ohhh,   to go   to the Faery Glen.

In a thunderous roar from the cushioned bank
Emilita clings ferocious...
for the bulb that grows;
she stares at innocence perched on a toadstool but
the King of Mist ferocious and furious
delves into a dire raging fury!

And the clouds crawl over
and the sun hides low
and the trees never sleep their gold!

Emilita Emilita wild with child
clings to the river bank
a bulb about to flee
tucked under a bramble
whispering a song
whispering to the Son of the Ocean
She sees love gushing blood on the ocean's floor.

Oh Son of the Ocean
tame the human wild
plunge forth your power
with your glacial sword,
for Emilita is in danger
the Snow God is angry
and the Soldiers of the Sea
flee along the river bank
flee along the sea.

To shake the wrath of innocence
to shove the silken evil
to hypnotize the harps.

Now in the uprooted bulb of loving to not love there is no back door.

No more dreaming in the universe ever.
Ever.

The King of Mist in his wrath has banished
dreaming cast his spell.
Is Emilita in hell?
If this unborn wildchild is not born
dreaming will no longer blow the horn.

No more dreaming in the universe ever.
Ever.

Where are the Soldiers of the Sea?
They have fled the glen.

Emillta
holding on to a blade of grass
driven by a thunderous wind
as a little bulb beyond wonder
shouts out to the
Soldiers of the Sea;

Soldiers of the Sea
my belly pokes the truth
my heart it bleeds in pain
and my tongue a hungry innocent.
I am banished from the Faery Glen
where wonder lives in puddles
and my love has been hacked off and butchered!

And now I hang
on this blade of grass
driven by a thunderous wind
under the bulb of wonder.
There are no Soldiers of the Sea
they cannot come and rescue me
I'll never return to the Faery Glen.

Ohhh   to go   to the Faery Glen
the wild with child Faery Glen
where the trees sleep gold
and the grass never grows old
Ohhh, to go   to the Faery Glen.

Where green whispering trees call out to me
all the ancient stories told
and the flesh of my bosom
never turns cold
and the cry of my soul never grows old.
Ohhh human man manity I cry out to thee
the King of Mist has banished me
from the whiteness of angels
from the wildness of wild grass
from the dewy hunger that hangs as a relish to all humankind
from the moan to harness all moans
from the softness under the sea
from the Seagod of Small Creatures
from the ancient wild child
from me.
So,   I call and command   that the Soldiers of the Sea
come out to me
as I hang on my blade of grass
driven by the thunderous wind
Soldiers of the Sea
C'mere c'mere to meee.

And the ocean in a thunderous roar
shouts out Emilita Emilita
the blood from the floor
gushes out and up splashing,
and my blade of grass whistles in the wind
and the stars are shouting tomorrow tomorrow
the petals from the Seagod of Small Creatures shake in their skin,
the God of Snow flushes red.
The Son of the Ocean grows and grows into a giant human eye
upward and onward the battle goes
the waves plunge and they plunge
and the Soldiers of the Sea they came to me!

Oh Soldiers of the Sea
drenched in their chains and buckets of coal
armed in the arms of ancient men
Emilita hangs on her blade of grass cold

driven by a thunderous wind
with the bulb and the wild child.

All the soldiers grasp a breath
and they huff and they puff
a powderous potion of gaseous black coal
and the imminence of fire...
Redder and hotter than the ancient sun
whacks and plunges the ocean's highest wave in a thunderous roar
the King of Mist appears in the sky
holding a head of brown hair upsidedown backwards
the hair of humanity shall not enter the Faery Glen!

And the ocean leaps in fury
the Soldiers of the Sea gallop ferocious
One   two   three
they all jump with the buckets of coal and the chains of the world
the moaning seas gush and they gush
night and day smack one another
causing a fertile anguish
birth and death knock on the back door
and the blood that heaves
and the fire that blows
the thunderous rain belting the brave Soldiers of the Sea.

Emilita on her blade of grass driven by a thunderous wind
smacks and pokes shoves and smokes to the Valley of Angels,
even the angels are angry!
And they pop and open up the thunderous sky bellowing
they take offf their crowns and salute the Soldiers of the Sea
they summon the Son of the Ocean
a soft   moonbeam
appears in the sky
the Soldiers of the Sea in their chains
are cut open like wounds
Emilita shouts;

Oh live and love luxurious blood runs as passion on the ocean's floor!
Oh live and love luxurious blood runs as passion on the ocean's floor!
Oh live and love luxurious blood runs as passion on the ocean's floor!
Oh live and love luxurious blood runs as passion on the ocean's floor!

Don't worry we are the Soldiers of the Sea!

The carnage that crumbles
the dawn breaks bold
the moon sweats a chickenpox fever
and the angels sing a song:
Oh chain oh chain
to the Soldiers of the Sea
give us light give us hope
we want to smoke with the stars.

And the King of Mist rises again
shaking his fist like giant hammers
stamping his feet with a burly scowl
he dreams of women in chains
and with a supreme ultimate howl
splattered in blood
he flings himself upsidedown backwards
into the belly of space...

And the Soldiers of the Sea are free
the Soldiers of the Sea are free,
and the Valley of Angels hum in their bosoms
the Valley of Angels hum in their bosoms,
And the dreaming in the glen is set free
And the dreaming in the glen is set free,
Emilita on her blade of grass driven by the thunderous wind

is sitting in the belly of the Faery Glen
with her new born wild child and the Seagod of Small Creatures.

SOLDIERS OF THE SEA DRENCHED IN THEIR CHAINS AND BUCKETS OF COAL

I woke with the Soldiers of the Sea, drenched in their chains and buckets
of coal,

there were daisies

Oh Soldiers of the Sea, on their ship of night dark, humanity saves reality
from sleep tinkers.

Save sinking ships aghast huddle together
Soldiers of the Sea

c'mere c'mere to meee

they jump to save all the drowning fears,

jump with their chains and buckets of coal
to save   a landscape   half dream

to propel forward in the fire of sea
imagination   fishes out   on a net

TRAPPED

You ask
trumpeted on demand
lingers you're lagging   tongue
trapped
between
sex and a bus home.

WANDERING DARK

Those wandering dark companions that drop in the night
feed us away toward back again
through space thoughts of time
defines us wholly among ourselves and I.
We may never know
vastness stretching
long hallways climb
wounded childhood that hangs in anger.

Oh discarded womb whose hero knows not themselves or fate.

Wandering through twilight red
this blackness called night
plays dripping , drenched in promise dressed
sweet as rain, wind blows;
I know those wandering dark companions that stand before
so close among our boundaries where lovers come and go!

Beyond the wild times chasing snow in silent streets, fate
a golden hammer tiny
creature sheltering from bliss curling caressing
stretch another's skin
anticipating departure soft reassures
our presence growing smaller,

the distance of our selves
flashes as childhood and future fornicate
companions of the dark bright of others as we
stand before hovering
getting the fear locates and then;

Chasing us the closeness comes growing twilight wanders on
out lost in the selves that we thought we once knew
or may never know
or know not know
do we ever fully know?

A dark stranger
lying alongside one another sleeping.

Almost sleeping in protection
those wandering dark companions disappear
shadows of our sleeping selves
isolated creatures of our own bodies
screaming silence a space that has no tongue!

PETTICOAT PETTICOAT

Petticoat petticoat
tales of woe
this time   this time
there's
no
where
to
gooooooo

SOONFLOURSUN

Ohnights whichwander me wallowon
forever everthinpieces of strawblowembers
uponmemories of legshanging overstars.
In the wardrobeofyouth Iventure inandthrough
neverto returnbutbreak allthe candiesthatbubble
methrough whimwishes wherefall andstops
asablister flakepokeme intheeyes awkward.
Frustrationblows asadomino snowballgallops
forward afieldrakes
ohhhhhsoon floursun
findme
find m eeee
find m eeeeee
the
S
U
N

THAT SWEET SLEEP

Oh sweet sleep
that dreams on the skin of kings and the arms of beggars
begging presence
where they know or may not know
distance or hope that covets them;

       onward —
a spring day
diluting the child's own cloak that carries
him toward the blind spot.

The blind spot where there is no sweet sleep.

Swift a foot the King of Sea travels smartly to cover
a distance where unusually shaped objects gather close and
come toward him as warriors
they rise and rise from the earth that has buried them
once.

Mighty warriors dressed in cloaks descend among
the sullen moon, surrendering sea
where they show their disruptive darkness lonely lingers
among tongues and time of seed,
hovering toward the back black roads and bends.

They know where they are going
these warrior gods of wounded countrysides that lie
forgotten and discarded where no man has house or land and
families are non-existent,

only distant strangers hanging on the trees as leaves
smitten and dismissed,
elemental bearings, warriors bidable by night seeking
bodies and minds to surrender themselves;

mere mortals of women and men troubled bones in bags
fleeing their own blood in the sweet sleep of night — no
nothingness.

Warrior-gods plagued disenchanted walking the earth mild
no;
ferocious not in retreat
warrior-gods dispel red and white foam from the sea
wild, banished in bitterness
mere children of the sweet sleep of night find a shore that
doesn't despise likeness of their once own bodies no longer
their own.

Where they once boasted their blood hysterical suggesting
hovels, they wheel their own bodies through
the darkness of that
           — sweet sleep calls night!

HOME HOME IF YA DON'T GO TO HEAVEN YOU'RE A HA'PENNY LATE

Childhood wire on a stringsing, nanny of diamond skirt

    you forgot to hang the children up to dry… do those dishes,

sticks of wishes that won't go away, a child lost, hay stacks that poke and
choke.

ohhh loopsong to heaven, hush and goo

liar liar childhood fire

        heaven hopes to dream

liar liar wishing well

        don't break the spell

a ha'penny wish
hush and blow when i go
don't burn my soul
child oh child ohhhh wishingwell, metropolis hell,
this is no disneydream but a
            delinquent dreammmm

IN THE JUKEBOX OF MY MIND

In the jukebox of my mind
I play songs
not love songs.

Tunes bury dead bones in sheds,
vacant rooms on outside hedges
lift ten hundred green bottles on orange mushroom walls
days of night dream, light, half light, half dream, half the night.

Then it breaks back to day, the love songs don't go away,

jukebox play the panic tracks
the piano has been drinking
voodoo child
I walk the line
people are strange
wish you were here
such a perfect day.
I play songs

farmers burst the tango sod
rappers dance a rubber boot
hookers pine the stranger broke
dreams pursue the hooolie night.

Jukebox play a song,
the sky lies naked in hooliemoon hair

and the song plays.

FLASK SECRET

Your naked chest pirandello
floats round my frightened
skin bites on....

Pigeons stare thru Alaskan
corridors spit buckets
whilst our bodies
galk in nights bitter brightness.

After
your face tumbles
uncaused
my frozen web curdles
momentarily
soft you open the stain in me.

MAKEMEDREAM

The moon
it wears a cloak
Ohhh soon coloured moon
discover my shame.

Deny me dress; disentangled dream
who knew you once?
So bliss descends amongst the weir
forsaken, banished for noooo ears.

For your cloak and bliss do make
some questioned, humbled   HESITATE.

Go onn mymoon in naked strait
swim you're anger — don't be late,
for when the light comes out nomore

death shall sip death shall roar!

Go shame go shame go dance withal
disassemble disinvent
some futuristic effer   scent.

HASTE — I bid you
moon with cloak
step me through the turquoise smoke
gather
gather
disenchanted dream
of light and dark — my ancient   BEAM.

Sweet slipslide moon makemedream

sweet slipslide moon makemedreammmm

MUSTARD HEAVEN

Sex, he says
bracketed blocked
among hunger
fried fish fingers
sizzle on.

Sex, he says
butter on fingers
scratch the groan
letter word stretch
against storm thighs
waits waits waits waits, she.

Sex, he says
hoan cowl
toward a spot
the shop is closed
the shop is closed
she croaks.

Sex, he says
lick the lips
Ohhhhhh, mustard heaven
hide the orgasm quick.

Sex is not a stock exchange.
Sex is not a stock exchange.

So, no she says
hammered
as her ear gallops
far inside
her darkened night ...

LOVE'S BLACK DOOR

Lonesome wild boy
dry me cold
an ancient story told;

I knew you once; again before
some unclosed country   some closed shore

your lips, dewy draw me in
your eyes, unmentioned, snows therein

I dream me daily, on before
gather soft loves black door.

Drift denies your colored reign
my face tumbles, know not my name
your loosened swoops give me sup
stop me, stomp me, give me puck!

I stand   a fool   bewildered eyes
a weary weakened lost mild child,
I stand befuddled at love's black door
under sunset, under shore.

No sun can shine to know me there.

Ponder on love's old floor
demand me this
a quandering kiss,
landscapes driven beneath skies
or skin wandering wide — sighs.

Draw my eyelids' open wool,
my skin that dreams your flesh to roar!

So

pucker   pucker
love's black door

pucker pucker
love's back door

THAT PINK LOVE POTION

That pink love potion
turns
to go on go on I gooooo.

It smothersun some months ago
it cannot go it cannot go,

it chuckles, burns and belly flaps
slinks among
waxed butcher wrap.

Wrapped in newspaper tied with rope
confused and lost
ready to grope.

Out among the tattered stars
down the muddied waters wide
licked and sucked
in the bee hive
drenched in the ancient tide.
But it arrives

on a battered bench

looped, pushed, mustered, nook
christened down
burdened up.

A vision pink that bursts apart
liquid liver from the start,

that pink
that pink
that pink
that pink
yesno

that pink love potion
turned
to snow

FROM FRIENDSHIP TO FIVE QUID

Yes yes yes yes yes
you
who dyed the roots of my hair red.

Yes yes yes yes yes
you
who shared cigarettes as night sucks
in the lonely bombay sapphire gin.

Yes yes yes yes yes
you
who gallivanted in gallant halls
triumphed in puny stalls
skinned the embittered tendrils
sincerity's road stretched
as an elastic band tight!

Yes yes yes yes yes
you
who baked the cherry buns
to feed the ideals of silly fools
burnt the cinders,

Yes yes yes yes yes
you
who sucked the honey of money
over the electric hill bill
for what...

Yes yes yes yes yes
you
who sooked the
manic panic attack pills
who kissed the embered lips
behind the stolen oak tree
for what...

Yes
from friendship to five quid!

HEROIN HITCHHIKE

Two bodies
wake bake
cuddle i
a heroin hitchhike.

Clump on
bruised begetmenots.

Two brothers cling
on whitewashland
brittle soldiers
carry
a honeyed needle.

Heroin hitchhike
needles in the sky with ash.

Christmas crumbs
two brothers love lost want to go away not of this place
GRABBED shoved bottled hooked
on
a heroin hitchhike.

Twodie
ona toilet floor

needles in the sky with ash,

liquid
death
leaves,

disturbed pangs across a universal floor
those of us left
such weeping scuttles, wears no mask

2brothers
in a sky of ash.

WOMEN WITH IRONS IN KITCHENS

You women with irons
with irons fions
you women with irons in kitchens.

You women who scrub
tubs of heaven,
who change dirt nappies,
give sudors
to groaning babies,
wash snow bottoms.

Oh women with irons
oh women with irons
oh women with irons in kitchens.

You women
pebbles of the earth
peb a peddle,
shampoo women
who grow on toes
on toes of a hen
pen a men.

Rebuff on the cuff
of the cuff ling lock.
Stop all clocks.
Stop all clocks.
Dump shampoo
dump j-cloths,
go on a row
to the giant scrap yard;

Where j-cloths, dishrags,
tea towels, kitchen roll, dettol
ajax, baking soda moda, irons,
ironing boards, commodes,
Mr. Proper, Mr. Clean, Mr. Machine,
itchy gritchy scratch attack, JOY!

Rump a dump to the
giant scrap yard
at the earth's bottom;

Shampoo women with irons in kitchens.

You'll always find them in the kitchen at parties.

You'll always find them in the kitchen at parties.

NOT.

Women on the verge
On the verge
Revolt.

BODY ON THE CURRAGH

There's a body on the Curragh.

Oh body on the Curragh
such questions
dip;

Were you loved, were you lost?

Body on the Curragh

on your way

did you dream
did you scream?

Dearest dreams

b
o
d
y

CHILDHOOD IN A HAZE

Childhood in a	haze
dream,	
childhood in a	craze scream
childhood	drive me wild
childhood save me	voodoo child.

That dark violent smoke that bends and descends on the youthful skin of
summer as winter shoves a thorn among the wounded children, the
motherless fatherless neglected children cling on bitten and frightened
by the dangling roads rush through the blue sky open, a gaze that lifts a
spit out to rift and thrift a life that floats bursting, goads forward an
unexplained dream, no one tells us the whispering or why it happens,
how it travels through the air, trees breathing in the brain so soft,
harmless at first only to grow round the sodden ground, seat in flight of
childhood hips, sing dark ferocious, a smothering sudden arabesque,
misunderstood misinterpreted, sign the signal attempt to discover
desperate the stars travel down the dark night mystery – wonder floats
across rivers, puddles winking through tomorrows of a new daylight.

But I did not know the terrifying force that I would be filled with
continually as I travelled from morning to night and back again. No one
destined to greatness among the smouldering sadness that fills the clouds
on those grey hobbled days no where, the wounded sun in light, am I the
peep in discontentment, here they come ready or not keep your place or
you'll be caught.

Caught, I was always caught, the whisper doesn't die close, until the night
a hungry horse chaotic in countryside inside the mind hips and bones of
childhood cling round the mulberry bush, that floats high up above the
world so high diamonds, I'm told diamonds, I want to live in that sky so
high, all is there hunched, crooked until the whisper goes away. Silence,
darkness, sound melts invisible puddle with no impression, intent fixes
onnn up above the world so high, whisper travel elsewhere under
terrified childhood hip hangs the explaining out to dry and still there's
why?

IF YA DON'T GO TO HEAVEN AMERICO IS GREAT

Dumped smack in the middle of metropolis; mental craze dream

promise promise
disney   scream

black dollar, dream, chocolate trip dream, size massive, colossal, size
revolutionized, legs, people, bodies, growing, consume, recycle, fantasize

leave the homeland, chase a fastfood rainbow

Oh abyss, bucketof sky —

hang your childhoood   out to dry
childhoood wire   higher higher

if ya don't go to heaven

Americo is great...

SUBURB

My body on a suburb
denial,
full stops
echoes
wasteland.

Naked landscape
in my head
dries itself on
buttercup kisses floatttttttt,

body on a memory stands a tourist
backward toward space
where
hushfeargrowsloud

sinks

separate.

Body on a memory stands at a bus stop
yellow.

Body on a memory stands at a bus stop yellow with no name.

Body on a suburb

choke —

pile up on some rubbish heap

s u bu r b

bodymemoryyellowstandfloatttts

n   o   w   h   e   r   e.

HOUSTON STREET

Houston street
6th Avenue
our legs
the sky's footsteps,

bumped down to
a frowning seaport building
a woman's arms
open a 5th floor window
of the Paris café

3 bar stools
stepping stones
of the water's
pleading edge,

east river lonely
reaches
its lily white arms out
ebbs you forth —

a moaning pier stands
east river
kisses the dock
you stand on
the pier's stump jump to seduction,

climbing
pier
in
the
city
cannot
climb
the
company
of
stars

THE SOUL OF THE BUTTERFLY

American dream
stitched to a big
pie in the sky
over stuffed
over baked
flaked chips of pastry
dropping
as melted down rain
an ignored storm
of gun shots
steaming cries
in all the passing eyes.

I walk across 57th Street
a bag lady
with bumping pink cheeks
sadly decorated
makeup her bomb.

Mashed potatoes
in a meaty stew of
homeless pear boned
weeds sleeping thru
a ghostly nightmare.

And I stand in the wake of the living
trying to catch in a net
hope swimming thru
melted colors of a passing butterfly
smacked greedily
into a giant green dollar bill.

M IS FOR MOTHER

Stop at a drop y' know
every road I know
you step with me.
Up hills cushioned
lost milk weed sips,
from a mother
my mother's breast.

I know your layers
of skin between mine flow,
bitter moments rock
gently cradle
between my hungry cries.

I know your sighs,
pebbles in mine eyes
sting clutch.
Rasp in the veins
particles of hair
as they turn;

I shall comb the rustles out.
Protect from the moon's solitude,
fuss grope
miles of despair
without!

I know cries
that embrace
lines of my hands
your hands.
Caress newborn wrinkles
in the quaking mouth
of a quested river.

I know shared cracks,
grey hovels
fold in you
memories,
as clothes pegs
pin in
my heart
your washing line.

IF MILK WANDERS

If milk wanders
milk me now
thumps
the heart
ankled,

beyond
blood lips
fluffed quiet
surrender
empty pillow.

If milk wanders
milk me now
summer
glass trembles
dissipates
lick my marmalade.

If milk wanders
milk me now
dover wild,
pile up pile on
pile up on
plentora
pluck
pluck
pluck the lost lily
pluck the last lily
p
l
u
c
k

BURNING STICKS

Your smell of burning sticks
I tumble
carouse round
oodle freckled
pinch.
Your smell of burning sticks
speaks of football
telly, bar stools
pop
a meter.

Your smell of burning sticks
floats round me
naked
as I root through some car boot sale;

curiosities, dwindle, objects cluster clatter
together, aimless, haphazard, jumbled
into one enormous
pandamonious
heap,
all scatter cluelessly
in a backdrop of grass and rain smoking.

Your smell of burning sticks
tickles a
lonely dark
ancient ache
in me

hangs

hanging

on a rusty nail in the sunset.

HIDING

I do not know you
even today
in the couch of your eye
lies fear.

I do not know you
in the pillows
of childhood
lies anger.

I do not know you
beneath your skin
of life
lies a heartbeat.

Yet you share
the house
of my life
eat from
the same table
your shoes next to mine
on the floor afraid
and you live and you live,

hiding from fathers.

BARBED WIRE IN BELFAST

Barbed wire in Belfast
comes to me
stokes my skin
a stained room
under.

Barbed wire in Belfast
speaks to me —
curse shout despise

break - shatter,
crush a friend's dream.

Barbed wire in Belfast
choke me.
Ancient troubles hang round my neck,
union jack, green white and gold,
a necklace perfect damned;

oh celtic jewel
a new tin foil,
fold my skin,
sold my skin
scream bloodshed at me!

I sit in a pub
behind Essex Wall
where bombs kill
there is a music
here,
cradled in wire
that kills
all
sound.

CONTENTS